Our Reflections

Our Reflections

Ron Baratono

Copyright © 2018 Ron Baratono
All rights reserved.

ISBN: 9780692147948

Table of Contents

Finding Faith	vii
Emotions and Jesus Christ	ix
Don't Be Afraid to Fall	xi
Keeping Things Real	xiii
To Date or Not to Date?	xv
Looking for Truth	1
Imperfect World	2
Reaching for God	3
Imperfect Man	4
God's Shield	5
Ocean Eyes	6
Her Smile	8
Half a Heart	9
A Woman's Love	11
My Sons	12
My Sisters	13
My Brother	14
Fortune and Fame	15

Quiet My Heart	16
The Wise Owl	17
Man's Needs	18
Lost Friendship	19
Committing to Your Truth	20
The Frozen Path	21
Dad's Star	23
The Garden Chair	24
Moments of Love	25
Shattered Ribs	26
Betrayed	27
The Right Fighter	28
Freedom of the Heart	29
Did You Love Me?	30
Ron's Quotes and Prayers	31
Biography	49

Finding Faith

Faith in God breaks down tunnel vision and leaves the lack of imagination for life's truth in the past. He will place you where you need to be in life, opening up freedoms in your mind and the most wonderful things you've ever dreamed of. Give yourself a chance to believe. All over the world, people serve God in their own ways. Pick a plan for yourself and begin. There's nothing lost reaching for Him every day; there's the everlasting strength you'll gain in your heart and mind. You deserve the feeling of faith. You deserve the peace of mind God's love has for you.

So many times we asked ourselves, "What are we searching for?" We run into situations we feel are hopeless, with a sense that we've lost ourselves. Maybe life hasn't gone the way you've planned, and you feel there's no way out. There are times you'll feel so alone and will be so overwhelmed that you won't be able to share the situation with anyone. Your faith can be with you every day of your life and won't allow tunnel vision or lack of imagination to flow through your mind. You deserve peace in your heart, and most of all, you deserve to be happy and rejoice with the truth.

Emotions and Jesus Christ

Right at this moment, quiet your mind and think about your life—no one else's, just yours. Why do we hope and why do we dream? Why do we bear the burdens in our lives, and why do we seek to enjoy so many pleasures? When we wake up most mornings, there's calm in our minds. As the day moves forward, our brains are filled with interaction, most of it not important to our well-being until an emotion is triggered. Emotions stick! I can still remember the boy who beat me up in kindergarten.

Emotions play such a huge role in our lives; many people don't like to show their emotions in public, afraid of how they'll look or the judgment they will receive when showing their feelings. Women will show their feelings more often than men. A man doesn't want to appear weak, but trust me, those emotions are there. I have found that dealing with the truth through Jesus Christ has helped me deal with these emotions by placing them in God's hands, out in the open, and it's all a reflection of love. Love for myself and a love for my faith.

When we go through different situations in life, many people don't grasp what they're feeling or what's bothering them. They just can't put their fingers on it. That's when therapy comes in. Have you ever seen a therapist and noticed how he or she wants you to talk first? Their first question is always "How did that make you feel?" Their whole concept is based on your emotions. We hope and dream for our emotional happiness. We bear burdens of emotional grief, and the pleasures we seek are for satisfaction and a meaningful life. Sometimes our emotions can get the best of us, but understanding our emotions through Jesus and allowing ourselves to place things in His hands make our lives more calm and wonderful places.

Don't Be Afraid to Fall

We've all tripped over our own feet accidentally and fell without hurting ourselves. Oftentimes we get up laughing, maybe a little embarrassed as the people around us chuckle after seeing that we're OK. This happened to me in the shopping mall, but I didn't get up. I just sat there for a brief moment, looking at the faces of the people wondering if I was hurt.

I continued to sit there and watch as the laughter never came, and the people stared, wondering if I was going to get back on my feet. It didn't take long before a security guard noticed me sitting there and rushed over. "Are you okay!?" he asked, reaching his hand out to help me to my feet. "I'm just fine," I replied. I could feel a tear rolling down my face as I just sat there gripping his hand.

People slowing gathered around, staring. "Are you sure you're okay?" he asked again. This time I said, "No." He looked at me without surprise; he had seen my tears. He managed to help me to my knees, but I wasn't going to stand up. At a glance, again I noticed even more people watching.

I could feel their stares; there I was, a grown man on my knees in the middle of the mall. The security guard was a big man, all dressed in blue with a gun strapped to his hip. It looked like he could pick me up and throw me ten feet if he wanted to. There was a kindness about him, so I told him my story. I didn't care that he was a complete stranger.

Looking up at the man, I explained, "My wife and I have been having problems for some time, and I haven't been home in a week. The separation is hurting the kids, and tomorrow I'm filing for divorce. It feels like my whole life is falling apart." Right at that moment, I thought for sure I would be asked to get up and leave. Instead, he knelt down next to me and told me, "My son is hooked on heroin, and I haven't seen him in a month. My wife and I don't know if he's dead or alive." We both began to pray as tears filled his eyes. Soon, others who were watching came over to pray; they all seemed to have stories of their own.

We all trip and fall accidentally in our journeys through life; there are also some things we can't control. Sometimes our falls don't cause injury. God is watching us all, and there will be times He brings us to our knees when He knows we need to pray in Jesus's name. Amen.

Keeping Things Real

It's not the type of building you're in when you worship God; it's whether you do it with all of your heart. It's not the size of the stove you cook with; it's the taste of the food. It's not the amount of money a person makes; it's how much he or she saves. It's not important for our children to have everything as long as they're happy. It's not the price of the clothes you wear as long as you're comfortable in them. It's never important to have a large number of friends, only a few quality ones. If a man doesn't have his family, then that man has nothing. Success is not about money; it's about happiness. If a person is drama-free, he or she must be completely alone. The healthiest relationships should be with our children. The strongest emotion is a mother's love. Just because you have beautiful things and popularity does not mean we should look up to you. There are many ways to be rich—spiritually, emotionally, physically, and financially. There's no higher freedom than freedom within your heart, a sense of peace in your life.

To Date or Not to Date?

We circle around a meaningful path in our minds, unsure if it's going to turn out the way we hope. There's that sense of fear that it could be a waste of valuable time. "Giving it another chance" is the dater's favorite line. Yet a large percentage of men and women are on dating sites seeking attention, something they desire more than a relationship. Women with their provocative pictures and men posting that brand-new Ford pickup truck. How can they get a fish on the line to fulfill the lack of attention in their lives? After all, he or she is rather attractive. This is why, once connecting with that person, he or she chooses to endlessly text or message until that person finally realizes that looking them in the eyes will never happen.

Some men and women can't find time to date; they have extremely busy lives with kids and work, but it's the thought of getting back out there, breaking redundancy, capturing that loving feeling, that's very intriguing. They once felt it, and wouldn't it be nice to feel that again? Let's not forget the person who dates for the sport of it, three dates a week. What an ego booster! So they think. Then there are the hopeful. These are the people, including myself, who believe that things happen for a reason and the basic foundation of our lives are the people we let in. I've said this before: "They don't have to stay," and they don't have to leave on bad terms. These are the people who teach us about ourselves—laugh, cry, or fall in love, we need these emotions to capture the true foundation of who we are and what we want in our lives. When true love comes, it will be enhanced because of reflections we've had along the way.

Looking for Truth

Looking for the truth
as it stares into my heart
those feelings of emptiness
a world that fell apart.

Those burdens of yesterday
lay scattered in my mind
tomorrow's yearn for happiness
might somehow pass me by.

At least I found the truth
through bitterness and pain
I'll stare into a hopeful heart
and try for love again.

Imperfect World

Happiness is a state of mind
when we live with no regrets
blaming one's self so randomly
the harder life could get.

The picture-perfect foundation
those smiles they often wear
we'll never know the pain they feel
frustration they can't bear.

Hidden from a daunting view
a house of broken dreams
landscape rest so perfectly
it's not the way it seems.

Pictures lay in shattered glass
hidden from the crowd
a purple moon shines darkness down
silence seems so loud

The sunshine that awaits you
can wash away your tears
regrets in an imperfect world
something we all fear.

Reaching for God

Reaching for God's light
as the darkness fills my mind
a meaningful surrender
can I get to Him in time?

Unaware of the darkness
as it creeps into my life
not holding on tight enough
to avoid the lonely nights

Reaching for His hands
warmth came rushing through
crawling for peace of mind
a place I always knew.

I'll never walk away again
His grace that came to be
this glorified surrender
God's love that's meant for me.

Imperfect Man

In the silence of the morning
I'll search for some regrets
the troubles that I caused myself
things I can't forget.

Always reaching for shattered dreams
that seem so out of sight
stumbling on a tattered past
that never turned out right.

Imperfect arms that reach for you
though Jesus lights my way
I'll pick myself up one more time
and live for Him each day.

God's Shield

The snow falls like broken glass
God shields us from the storm
the winter chill and quietness
a heart that once was torn.

Nature glitters morning light
brightness meets the day
beauty that surrounds the heart
feeling God this way.

Tears that fell so long ago
now frozen into love
snowflakes rest upon my heart
from Heaven up above.

Ocean Eyes

There's a smile when she speaks to me
while I try to catch my breath
imagining her lying next to me
almost scares me half to death.

I'm supposed to be the strong one
so I'll never let her see
that every movement that she makes
can bring me to my knees.

Her blue eyes are an Ocean tide
that's washed upon the shore
waves that rush into my heart
each one stronger than before.

I'm surrounded by this feeling
how lucky that I am
this woman God sent my way
makes me a happy man.

We'll wonder what the future holds
as the sun fades slowly down
water lands on the rocks
without a single sound.

Our Reflections

The Ocean seemed to carry
her blue eyes far away
along the shore my open heart
that's where it will lay.

Her Smile

The morning mist don't mean a thing
or the fog that blinds my day
there's a light that shines in her eyes
when she smiles that certain way.

Unsure of what the future holds
like an hourglass that's mine
the path of life and the haze it brings
seems brighter all the time.

My hopeful heart that's lying there
beating steady in her eyes
can she feel me reach for her
or will it take some time?

Through the mist I'll take another step
as her smile lights my way
holding on to hopefulness
and her smile that makes my day.

Half a Heart

You'll find happy days, they told the woman whose heart had been torn apart. The man who left wasn't right for you. God knew that from the start. There's a happy time that waits for you beyond that closing door. Everlasting promises, love, and so much more.

Relationships aren't a buffet where you pick and choose what's right. It's a promise accepting everything from dawn until evening light. The man who left used half a heart; in the end, that's clear to see. You'll find the love that waits for you—it's the love that's meant to be.

Your confidence lays weak as you think about the past. Wanting someone who doesn't want you is sometimes hard to grasp. There's a treasure he walks right past without reaching for the Gold. This will be that man's loss and something he can hold.

Pick yourself up, my dear, and take a good look at your pain. Did you really want just half a heart that came through pouring rain? There's Hope beyond that closing door through the tears you'll find your way to a man who deserves that loving heart you give each and every day.

A Woman's Love

The world awaits her loving heart
through her eyes she'll hide some tears
you'll never know how hard she tries
when you asked about her fears.

The strength of a woman
it's there from the start
unlock the feelings deep inside
you'll find a gentle heart.

Her touch is like an ocean breeze
lying naked in your mind
you'll rush to her for tenderness
to have her by your side.

My Sons

Deepest love on a mountaintop
I'll stand proudly in the wind
flowing with everlasting love
before each day begins.

All my reasons for the life I lead
while the sunshine meets the sky
warmth that beats in a father's heart
two young men who are mine.

Days pass, the sunset fades
time goes rushing by
darkness holds a moonlit night
two stars still fill my eyes.

Looking back at the blessings
God placed upon my door
my young men are the largest ones
I couldn't ask for more.

My Sisters

Precious gifts are my sisters
for the dreamer of dreams
a guiding light that follows
what the sunset truly means.

Placed upon a sandy beach
the righteous walk for me
protected by unconditional love
staring out to sea.

Never lost or uncertain
standing there alone
God's gift from heaven
they're there to guide me home.

These women in my heart
their love is so much more
my sisters are my treasure chest
God placed upon the shore.

My Brother

Reach into my heart
for memories that last
you'll find a painted picture
of a warm and happy past.

The rugged roads we traveled
at times without a care
through the seasons of our lives
I'm blessed that you were there.

There's a mountain filled with trust
and a kindness in your eyes
will always be together
like the sunset fills the skies.

Painted shades of a wonderful blue
will rest upon my heart
my brother is that special man
I could never live without.

Fortune and Fame

The wallet full of dollar bills
a purse that's full of smiles
feeling like that's all you'll need
but only for a while.

The bitter pill you swallow
could make life a better place
the chain of pearls around your neck
the happiness it makes.

Attention can be a lonely place
some fake and unforeseen
smiling hands that reach for you
to give them what they need.

Those smiles fade away from view
when they leave the mansion gate
It's happiness you're searching for
that's something they can't take.

Quiet My Heart

Quiet my heart, dear lord
while they speak the frozen words
transparent voice their insecure
it's advice that's barely heard.

Tongues sharp like a broken knife
you've heard this all before
advice about what you need
you didn't ask for more.

Explaining yourself like a wooden gate
swinging rusty in the wind
hoping that the hinges break
you listen once again.

Frozen words with a chilling pain
while they leave you in the cold
it's recognition they're searching for
with advice that's growing old.

The Wise Owl

The fear of Confrontation
that's written on your face
searching for the words to say
the ones you can't replace.

Thinking so very deeply
as the anger reaches its peak
catching yourself from falling
into words you shouldn't speak.

The Wise Owl comes out
as the rain comes pouring down
clouds appear above your head
so they speak when you're around.

They look for certain flaws
where the Wise Owl feels safe
In pity you pray for them
with God, your fears erase.

Man's Needs

The needs of a man are always met
when it falls upon his soul
hungry heart, a loving touch
this way to make him whole.

Greed of a man is an endless search
as he staggers with each step
paralyzed with obsessive thoughts
the greed is never met.

The difference of need and greed
we can find within our faith
a simple prayer to meet our needs
in God's loving hands of grace.

Lost Friendship

Friendship lost as the sunset fades
the summer breeze is gone
darkness fills the sky most days
like a never-ending song.

The pieces always missing
that may never be returned
an open heart of memories
bridges that were burned.

Those distant Rhymes of happiness
echo softly with God's love
a friendship of a lifetime
sent from up above.

That summer breeze turned into rain
I'll search for another Rhyme
wonderful memories lay in my heart
stay hidden in my mind.

Committing to Your Truth

Commit to your truth
while you reach for inner strength
the fears that rest upon your soul
put them in one place.

Don't keep them on the surface
as you stare out into the world
there's nothing you can't accomplish
that voice you always heard.

You're stronger with the truth
a commitment in your mind
being all you're meant to be
these fears you push aside.

Buried deep inside your heart
is the fear that causes you pain
lost and now forgotten
it's the truth that will remain.

The Frozen Path

A long walk down a frozen path
glancing in the woods
thinking of the time gone by
exhausted, there I stood.

Thinking of my memories
the smiles and the pain
lost in thought of yesterdays
it then began to rain.

The winds seem to bite my flesh
through the bitterness and cold
I wandered off in sadness
a young man growing old.

Now lost and uncertain
where the path began
praying for Jesus desperately
to somehow take my hand.

Looking through frozen branches
was my path to make it home
the beautiful sound of silence
when you know you're not alone.

Our paths aren't always easy
reaching for God above
those frozen branches in my heart
now melted into Love.

Dad's Star

Listen to my broken heart
as it beats inside my chest
Dad is slowly drifting home
though I truly have been blessed.

Heaven awaits the greatest man
who kept me from the cold
he raised us kids, his the work of life
we watched him growing old.

I'm trying not to cry today
as I hold my family tight
letting go is hard to do
but things will be all right.

There's peace with every breath he takes
like the stars that shine so bright
our clouded hearts will heal in time
Dad's star will fill our nights.

The Garden Chair

The garden chair sits empty
God took our father home
Dad is watching all of us
so we'll never be alone.

We miss you, Dad, your loving ways
the time we had you here
it doesn't seem long enough
as we wipe away our tears.

Your work of life surrounds us
the loyalty you've taught
love each other with all your heart
that's what family's all about.

The garden gates opened wide
you walked in without a care
God is standing next to you
with your brand-new garden chair.

We miss you, Dad.

*Special thanks to my sister Kathleen Baratono Jones
for assisting with this poem. Hugs, sis!*

Moments of Love

Surrounded by those memories
trapped behind a smile
they carried away my heart
then spoke sadly for a while.

The time we shared
and the man I've become
this strength, love, and wisdom
can never be undone.

Walking slowly into darkness
can I carry the weight you knew?
I'm cluttered with untamed thoughts
not sure of what to do.

My soul cries for freedom
in a heart that's not so clear
it's those memories of love
they'll always keep me here.

Shattered Ribs

Take a bullet for the small crowd
wounded beneath their screams
hanging on with shattered ribs
they drag you from the scene.

Gingerly they walk in silence
gloating quietly with their thoughts
building accolades without self-doubt
they'll never live without.

Listen to their spoken words
while they brush against your mind
obsession with heroic tones
how they got to you in time.

In a quiet room, you'll feel the hurt
while they live without a care
shielding them from shattered ribs
you were the one that was standing there.

Betrayed

Streetlights shine a yellow blur
like bee stings in the cold
lifeless trees cry for help
each time the wind could blow.

That small bridge in the distance
burns slowly all the time
quiet thoughts are impossible
to ease your worried mind.

The alley hides a shadow
someone lurking in the night
winter chill wraps around your heart
something just not right.

Staring through broken glass
bees sting your bitter face
the bridge will burn forever
that distance can't erase.

The Right Fighter

A black rose lies on a wooden shelf
like their heart when it's distressed
beauty fades as the petals fall
life becomes a mess.

Blinded by an inch of pride
their screams, a blood-red face
look deep into a musty mirror
a reflection with no disgrace.

Both feet standing on shaky ground
in a trench they're sinking fast
barking out the righteousness
hoping it will last.

Petals are gone on the black rose
It's turned ugly after time
reflection from the musty mirror
vanished in their minds.

Freedom of the Heart

My heart holds a secret
beating inside my chest
shadows run within my mind
when life seems such a mess

Across the bridge is a small town
where I'll rest in bed alone
thoughts of her rarely cross my mind
she'll never make it home.

Hints of sorrow roll off my skin
sadness still rushes by
dark clouds fill an empty space
I'll stop to close my eyes.

Awaken to the real truth
the freedom in my heart
thank you, Lord, for giving me
a brand-new place to start.

Did You Love Me?

Did you want me
or just stay with me awhile?
Was the word "forever"
ever written in your smile?

With all the pain I'm going through
it's hard to think what I should do
I only wish I had a clue
did you love me?

The way I'm feeling
lost without your smile
you're going to tear our world apart?
Then give me a place where I can start.

Please come and tell me
what I don't really want to hear
you want your freedom
while our memories stand still.

If it's over then let me face the truth
clear my mind of memories
rid my thoughts of what could be
I only wish that I could see.
Did you love me?

Ron's Quotes and Prayers

Some people are so afraid of failure, they won't take that first step toward success. It's that first step that begins to put that fear of failure behind you.

It's always the person who's around the least who has the most to say. Proving he or she knows it all is not on his or her agenda. Their objective is to desperately plug back in with the people they've created distance between.

Rid your thoughts of monetary success on a grand scale. Lead every day with love for the people around you; it's those riches that will return your way that have the most value.

Don't fall into a relationship that not only makes you unhappy but also stifles your hopes and dreams to better yourself and move forward in life.

It's the little things we do for others that mean the most, freeing them up to take care of something else in their lives. You've sacrificed your own time and given it to someone else! Giving a person more time is the most valuable gift of all.

Don't feel undeserving for the success you've worked for. Don't sabotage your own progress in fear that you can't live up to how awesome you really are. Wear your blessing proudly and pass your goodness on to everyone you meet. It will be the open hearted and the joyful minds that recognize your loving spirit and dedication.

Sometimes our minds go wandering off into darkness, imagining a possible situation that could be unpleasant or stressful. We often wonder in fear how we will face this. Never fear; most situations turn out the exact opposite of what we thought.

Never tolerate people who invade your private space for their own personal gain. They have no conscience. They're not friends and need to be cast aside forever.

The reason many people stay single is that they've lived their lives in peace for a number of years and they don't want anything to change that. Juggling fear and peace of mind is a balancing act.

We're all just a second away from our lives completely changing. Find what makes you happy right now, and get rid of what doesn't.

The series of events we get involved with will dictate how our lives unfold. Walk away from unwanted drama. Take steps toward kindness, regardless of your pride. Build your own bridge to freedom.

Many times in life, we encounter a problem or situation that makes us feel unconformable, so we circle around the problem in our minds, creating life distractions. In reflection, we should focus our thoughts on the solution to that problem, freeing our minds from the negativity it's caused.

Dear God,

We asked that today you begin to unlock any darkness that's buried deep within us—the darkness we haven't been able to express to anyone. Please bring to the surface this sadness. We ask dear God to give us the strength to speak out so we can find peace in life and freedom in our hearts. In Jesus's name, amen.

There will be people in your life who will try to plan your future; these are the ones whose futures are the most uncertain.

I'd rather walk with a bit of depression than chase after a drug and lose my soul.

Recognize the signs: these perpetual questions and the need for control. Never be a part of someone else's obsession. Let them carry it alone with their snakeskin smiles. These are the people who hold their hands out and they're as cold as their hearts.

With all our reasons for living! Through our love and laughter, there's an unmistakable truth. The most valuable love in the world is a healthy relationship with our children.

Being a good parent requires being an outstanding salesperson. Direct communication and motivating our children or young adults with our ideals isn't easy. It's a lifetime job and job of a lifetime.

Feel pity for those with insecurities that rest heavy on their shoulders. They'll take every opportunity to negatively judge others. They speak with sadness in their voices, searching for something, anything, to make their lives feel just a little bit better.

There are days we all live with defensive thoughts in our minds. Unless we lose these thoughts, we can't totally be ourselves and enjoy life's freedom of the heart.

I think we all keep irritating situations in our heads too long, until we finally realize they're taking up valuable space.

Jealousy is a normal human emotion. When people act on that emotion, they then become haters.

Many people seek popularity and want everyone to know their names. It's not important for everyone to know your name; it's important that some of the people you know don't forget your name.

Regrets are a terrible thing to live with, but if we take a good look at them, some are not regrets at all—they're situations that taught us a valuable lesson. Don't be so hard on yourself. It's not a perfect world.

Life can be hard at times. People can be hard on each other. Being hard on yourself is completely unnecessary.

There's a reason we'll all end up with just a handful of true friends in our lives. These are the people who have taken the time to look at our hearts, so despite any flaws we have, they're forever in our lives.

When I found God, forgiveness also found me.

It's when you feel low about yourself that others' actions and options will affect you. When you look at yourself as a confident person, it's then that you'll find the most peace and understanding. It's your world you have to live in, not theirs.

Sometimes the situations we are the most afraid of, such as a commitment, are the very worst emotions for us. It holds our heart at bay in fear. When we start fresh with strength and an open mind, it breaks us out of the shattered glass of our past failures and allows us to find hope. Without hope, we're settling for less than what we really desire.

Dear God,

I asked that you clear my mind of any negative thoughts so my heart can run free, so I may look at the world with a clearer understanding of your beautiful creation. Cleanse my heart, dear God, so I may always look through the wonderful light you shine upon us. In Jesus's name, amen.

There are many ways to be wealthy, and there are many wealthy people who are very poor. Success is not about money; it's about happiness, inner peace, and loving yourself. Happiness and inner peace can come from your faith in God, and loving yourself is part of His plan.

In your heart, there's a way around the critics, minimizers, and judgmental people who hurt you when you understand that their self-confidence is very low. It's then that you can pray for them, that they find peace and allow all righteousness to come from Jesus Christ. Amen.

There would be a lot fewer broken hearts when a relationship fails if people would understand that there's no reason to want someone who doesn't want you. Never allow yourself to feel half empty when you deserve a relationship that will fill your heart with happiness.

Set out to be the person you know you can be. Thinking about it and talking about it is the first step. If you can imagine it for yourself, then you can do it.

The plan God has involves not just us as individuals but also the people who share part of our lives. Jesus was never alone; there were always people around Him. He had friends, followers, and people He could depend on. Never be afraid; someone wants to listen in your time of need. Reaching our hands out, especially when we're hurting, has the power to heal our hearts.

May there never be a haze over your eyes preventing you from looking at your life just the way you planned it. Through the bumps, twists, and turns in your journey, let it make you wiser. Embrace life's lessons with gratitude and appreciation and then move forward with an open heart and mind.

Always think and always dream. Wonder what's around the next corner for yourself, and don't be afraid to go there, but most of all, love. Loving yourself and the people around you is the easier path through life. It will bring you around that corner and to places you've never been before.

Never give up on your dreams! When you're good at something, and there's love in what you do, passion will always bring success.

Starting your day with anger is like locking yourself in jail. The outside world is enjoying life while you're locked in your own frustration.

The greatest compliment in the world is your adult children telling you they had a wonderful childhood.

We all have our times of anger. It's when we hang onto that anger that it becomes a slow poison to our hearts and minds.

It's nice to begin each day with an open mind, but a wonderful fulfillment will come with an open heart.

The most important influence in all our lives is love. If we're never taught to love, then showing and accepting love becomes difficult.

Every lie a person tells is an emotional dead-end road that puts weight on the heart. Satisfaction is always in the truth.

Just because a child doesn't have both parents raising him or her doesn't mean that child becomes half the person he or she was meant to be. One wonderful parent can love enough for two, and love will always be the biggest influence in a child's life.

Dear God,

I surrender myself to you. All that I am right now and all I'll ever be I leave in your hands. I understand that my life will not be perfect; there are things I must learn along the way. I'm asking for you to continue to remind me that you are the one in control. It's because I'm not perfect that I'll need these reminders. Please allow me to create joy in my life through your loving hands. In Jesus's name I pray, amen.

We're going to mess up in life. We're all going to do things and wonder why we did something so stupid. There're going to be times we say things that leave us feeling regretful. We're going to feel mad at ourselves and even ashamed at our own actions. Never be too proud to say, "I'm sorry" or "I love you." These are easy words that strengthen our hearts and give us peace and wisdom.

Why wait for later when there might not be a later? Why wait for next time when there might not be a next time? We all have just today to express our love. If no one ever told you they loved you, then now's the perfect time to liberate yourself—break that cycle and express yourself.

When the end comes for us in life, we will all be remembered by how much we loved.

It's not ever easy telling people what they don't want to hear. Because we love them! There will be times when we have to do things in life that will break our own hearts.

Faith in God is a promise that we're never alone, that there's a higher power that will look over us in times of despair. If people can just grasp this, even as an idea, they'll soon find that it's not just an idea but the truth to a more meaningful life.

If we're constantly trying to do the right things and for the most part help others, then we're having a conversation with God and we don't even realize it.

Never make an excuse for being yourself; no one's going to do it better.

Unless we can predict the future, we shouldn't be worrying about things that haven't happened yet. We can place these thoughts in God's hands and then let them go.

Seeking revenge is like reaching out for your own personal turmoil; it's never worth it. Righteousness will always come through Jesus Christ.

Demonstrating verbal kindness looks better on everyone no matter what the situation. There's a peace in the heart of the kind person who handles everything with love.

Having happy kids is far more important than anything they'll ever accomplish. Without happiness, success and contentment are always hard to reach.

Feel pity for the people who judged you rudely, for they are selfish in their judgment, trying to make their lives feel just a little bit better. It was never about you—it was all about them.

It will be God who brings out the peace in our lives and a calm in our hearts.

We can decide our fate every day; when we love, we will be loved.

With God's help, in the grasp of addiction you'll find the truth. When we understand this and God's purity, then true healing can begin.

None of us are perfect, so a true friend will never look for defects in you as a person; it won't even cross his or her mind. Your happiness will be his or her main concern.

Sometimes a goal in life we're striving for seems dim or becomes unreachable. Direction has suddenly changed so fast we're left with aimless thoughts and confusion. Don't be troubled! You've proved to yourself that you have the drive. Your new direction will come with patience. Each of us needs time to rest our hearts and minds before we reach the next mountain.

I think the greatest sound in the world is hearing one of your children singing when they think no one is listening.

If you desire romance, then give some—it's equally heartwarming. There are many ways to satisfy one's heart and feel special.

People will stop trying to prove they're something special when they finally realize they're already unique in God's creation.

Just a simple prayer today, for those who are sick or going through darkness of any kind. Dear God, we ask that you place your healing hands on the shoulders of our friends and loved ones who are suffering and relieve them of these hardships. In Jesus's name, amen.

For all the things we do in our lives and the people who surround us, it's family and those few loyal friends that God has blessed us with.

We all have anger in our hearts at times from past or even present situations. These thoughts hurt one's self more than anything. Without the effort of washing those from our minds, there can be no inner peace.

How we think is so important. There has to be a time when we stop just dealing with life and think about enjoying it.

I'm surrounded by beautiful sounds: my son singing in his room and a gentle rain. There are so many simple pleasures God gives us; we just have to listen for them.

Making each other's lives easier is true love. Enhancing each other this way is what makes a wonderful relationship.

Each day we hold things in our hearts; sometimes these things are heavy. Carrying God's grace with us each and every day lightens life's load.

In our quest for happiness, many times we evade the truth and remain unhappy. The truth lies within our hearts, regarding our faith, family, and inner peace. To love yourself is the largest truth you'll ever have. It's there where happiness begins.

The frustration of not knowing which way to turn in life is similar to a traffic jam. You're stuck! Don't you feel relief when the cars start rolling? Look at life this way: pick a path and see where it leads. Bring God's grace with you so you're not alone. You'll find that the frustration has been lifted and your search has begun. It's all in Jesus's name, amen.

You never know when someone will come into your life and change things, for good or bad. Let them in. They don't have to always stay, but human interaction is the pinnacle of life's lessons.

There's calm in each and every day, we just need to practice reaching out for it.

We all have a different answer to what defines our happiness and fulfillment, but for all of us it begins with inner peace. Without inner peace, happiness and fulfillment are hard to reach.

People live with fear, all kinds of it. Why don't we just let it all go? It has to be the biggest waste of time we all spend.

Right on the other side of our fears reside hope and happiness. We get stuck in our lives, afraid to walk over there where it's a much kinder place.

It doesn't cost anything to be a good person, and yet there are toxic people around us who will try to tax our lives.

The worst thing about being unhappy is not being strong enough to leave the situation.

One of the most exciting things in life is when you can't get enough of learning something you love.

Sometimes in life we must slowly distance ourselves from people and places we feel uncomfortable. Don't feel bad; feel free.

It feels good not to think about anything that wears on me. We all need that kind of room in our lives.

When we choose to love people and the wonderful things around us, it always puts us one step above the people who choose not to. There's a peace we'll carry in our hearts—that feeling of being worthy of all situations.

A meaningful life comes with the health, happiness, and productivity of our children, our family, and ourselves. So many people get their wires crossed seeking material goods, the things that make them feel better, as a means to happiness. The comfort of knowing our loved ones are healthy and happy is the treasure we should seek. That's where happiness rests for us, laying there for us beyond measure.

There's calm in my mind in the morning. A peacefulness that feels nice. A two-mile walk and prayer, then watering the garden, is relaxing for me. At the end of the day, I've reflected on my social interactions and wondered which of these interactions had purpose for a more meaningful life. I believe that with the presence of love and hope, we truly benefit spiritually. These are two emotions that make our lives more meaningful—not just love for God and ourselves but also love for the people around us, allowing hope and happiness to rest in our hearts. In the last few years, I've tried to be a calmer person in my mind and found it much easier with my love for Jesus Christ. I feel wonderfully honored to get the opportunity to write for you. Thanks for reading. God bless you and your family.

Biography

Ronald David Baratono was born in Detroit, Michigan, and is the second of four children. From 1984 to 1985, Ron directed *The Blarney Stone Show*, broadcast on Wayne Cable Television. From 1985 to 1990, Ron often performed community and dinner theater in Michigan.

Ron hired into the Auto Co. in 1977 at the age of eighteen, where he worked for thirty years. During that time, he still followed his passion for writing and acting. Ron studied at Northwood University and received his bachelor of business administration in 1995 while working full time.

He is the author of the personal nonfictional short story "Family Reflections" and of poems such as "My Life," "Dear

Jesus," "The Storm," "Dark Clouds," "God's Strength," and "My Sadness." In addition, he has quotes that are read worldwide. This is Ron's second publication. His first book, *The Writings of Ron Baratono*, was published in March 2015.

Ron is also a dad, which he considers the most rewarding job there is. He is the proud father of two wonderful adult young men, who are the highlights of his life. Ron retired from the Auto Co. in 2007 at the age of forty-eight. Today he continues to follow his passion for writing and acting, appearing in numerous films, including Disney's *Oz the Great and Powerful*.

www.ingramcontent.com/pod-product-compliance
Lightning Source LLC
Chambersburg PA
CBHW031429290426
44110CB00011B/588